THE TAPESTRY COLLECTION

FESCUE *by Marie Wallin*

5

RYE *by Marie Wallin*

COUCH *by Sarah Hatton*

HEATH *by Sarah Hatton*

LIBER

HOLM

MEADOW *by Sarah Hatton*

MILLET *by Marie Wallin*

12

MARSH *by Marie Wallin*

FOXTAIL *by Sarah Hatton*

BERTIE GLOVES *by Sarah Hatton*

GALLERY

FESCUE *by Marie Wallin*
Pattern page 28 Main image page 4

FOXTAIL *by Sarah Hatton*
Pattern page 43 Main image page 14

HEATH *by Sarah Hatton*
Pattern page 22 Main image page 8

MILLET *by Marie Wallin*
Pattern page 31 Main image page 12

COUCH *by Sarah Hatton*
Pattern page 40 Main image page 7

RYE *by Marie Wallin*
Pattern page 36 Main image page 6

MEADOW *by Sarah Hatton*
Pattern page 28 Main image page 9

MARSH *by Marie Wallin*
Pattern page 26 Main image page 13

BERTIE GLOVES *by Sarah Hatton*
Pattern page 34 Main image page 15

FESCUE

by Marie Wallin

main image page 4 & 5

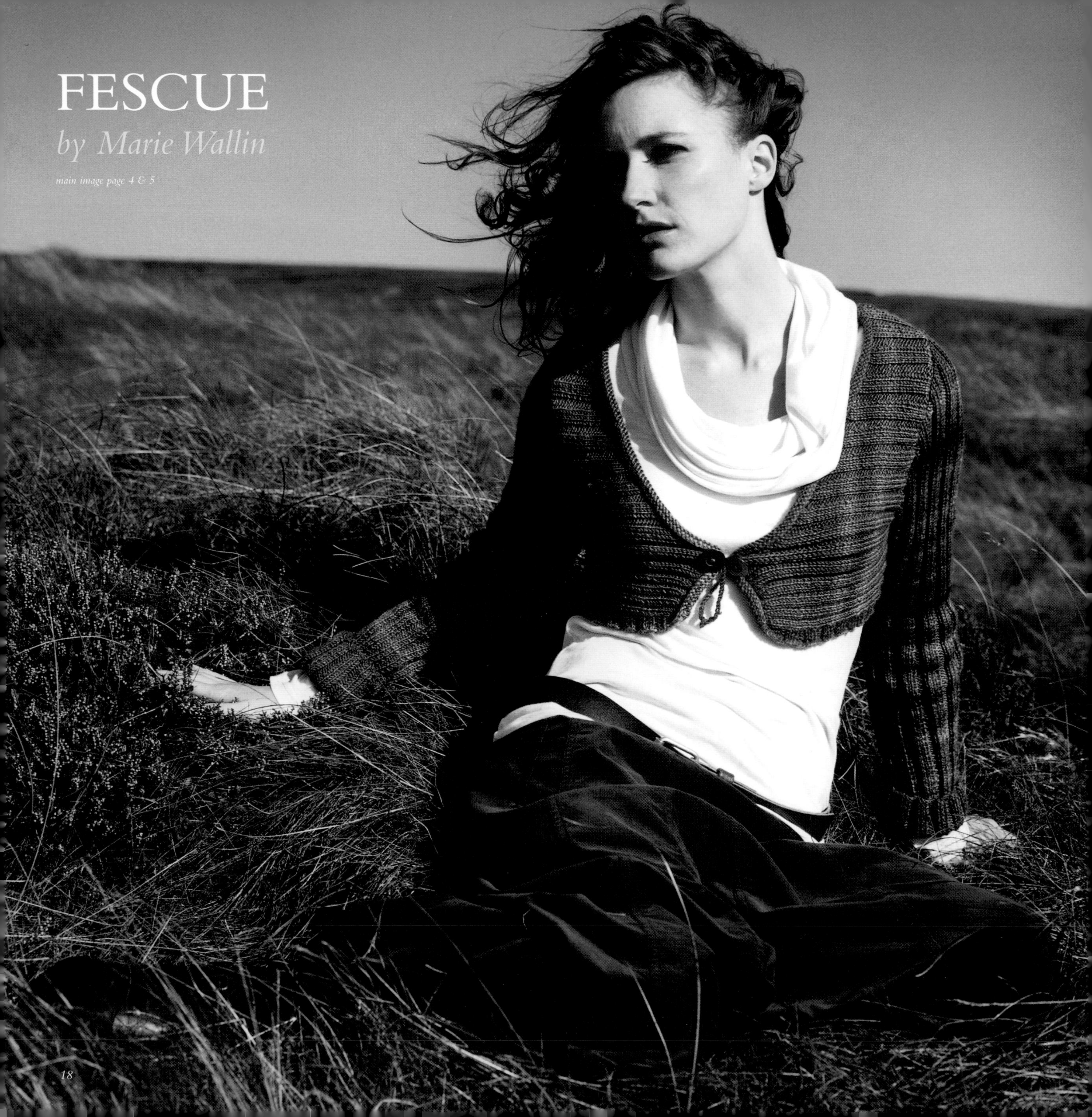

SIZE

	S	M	L	XL	
	8/10	12/14	16/18	20/22	
To fit bust					
	82–87	92-97	102-107	112-117	cm
	32-34	36-38	40-42	44-46	in

YARN

Rowan Tapestry

	8	9	10	11	x 50 gm

NEEDLES

1 pair 4mm (no 8) (US 6) needles
1 4mm (no 8) (US 6) circular needle
1 4.00 mm (no 8) (US G6) crochet hook

BUTTONS

2 x 00410

TENSION

30 sts and 30 rows to 10cm over 3x3 rib on 4mm (US 6) needles

BACK

Using 4mm needles cast on 135 [147, 165, 183] sts.
Row 1 – (RS) ★ K3, P3, rep from ★ to last 3 sts, K3.
Row 2 – ★ P3, K3, rep from ★ to last 3 sts, P3.
These 2 rows form 3x3 rib.
Work 34 [40, 40, 46] rows more in rib.
Shape armholes
Cast off 7 sts at beg of next 2 rows. 121 [133, 151, 169] sts.
Work 4 rows dec 1 st at each end of every row. 113 [125, 143, 161] sts.
Work 8 rows dec 1 st at each end of next and 3 foll alt rows.
105 [117, 135, 153] sts.
Work 5 rows dec 1 st at each end of next and foll 4th row.
101 [113, 131, 149] sts.

Work 41 [45, 47, 51] rows more.
Shape shoulders
Cast off 5 [6, 8, 9]sts at beg of next 2 rows. 91 [101, 115, 131] sts.
Cast off 6 [7, 8, 9] sts at beg of next 2 rows. 79 [87, 99, 113] sts.
Cast off 6 [7, 8, 10] sts at beg of next 2 rows.
Cast off rem 67 [73, 83, 93] sts.

LEFT FRONT (Worked from side edge to front edge)
Using 4mm needles cast on 32 [38, 38, 44] sts.
Row 1 – (RS) K2, ★ P3, K3, rep from ★ to end.
Row 2 – ★ P3, K3, rep from ★ to last 2 sts, P2.
These 2 rows set rib.
Work 3 rows more in rib, ending with WS facing for next row.
Shape armhole
Working all inc sts in rib proceed as follows:-
Work 6 rows casting on 2 sts at end of next and 2 foll alt rows.
38 [44, 44, 50] sts.
Work 4 rows casting on 3 sts at end of next and foll alt row.
44 [50, 50, 56] sts.
Work 2 rows casting on 4 sts at end of next row. 48 [54, 54, 60] sts.
Next row – (WS) Rib to end, cast on 44 [48, 50, 54] sts.
92 [102, 104, 114] sts.
Work 4 rows straight, ending with WS facing for next row.
Shape shoulder
Next row – (WS) Rib to end cast on 2 sts. 94 [104, 106, 116] sts.
Work 5 [5, 7, 7,] rows straight.
Next row – Rib to end, cast on 2 sts. 96 [106, 108, 118] sts.
Work 4 [4, 6, 6] rows straight, ending with RS facing for next row.
Shape neck
Next row – (RS) Cast off 9 [13, 15, 19] sts, rib to end.
87 [93, 93, 99] sts.
Work 1 row more.
Work 20 rows casting off 4 sts at beg of next and 9 foll alt rows.

FESCUE

47 [53, 53, 59] sts.

Work 8 rows casting off 3 sts at beg of next and 3 foll alt rows.
35 [41, 41, 47] sts.

Next row – (RS) P2, K3, (P3, K3) 1 [2, 2, 3] times,
(P1, P2tog, K1 K2tog) 4 times. 27 [33, 33, 39] sts.

Next row – (P2tog, K2tog) 4 times, P3, (K3, P3) 1 [2, 2, 3] times, K2.
19 [25, 25, 31] sts.

Next row – P2, K3, P3, K3, cast off rem 8 [14, 14, 20] sts.
Rejoin yarn to WS of rem 11 sts and P3, K3, P3, K2.
Cast off.

RIGHT FRONT (Worked from side edge to front edge)
Using 4mm needles cast on 33 [39, 39, 45] sts.

Row 1 – (RS) ★ K3, P3, rep from ★ to last 3 sts, K3.
Row 2 – ★ P3, K3, rep from ★ to last 3 sts, P3.
These 2 rows set rib.
Work 3 rows more in rib, ending with WS facing for next row.

Shape armhole
Working all inc sts in rib proceed as follows:-
Work 6 rows casting on 2 sts at beg of next and 2 foll alt rows.
39 [45, 45, 51] sts.
Work 4 rows casting on 3 sts at beg of next and foll alt row.
45 [51, 51, 57] sts.
Work 2 rows casting on 4 sts at beg of next row. 49 [55, 55, 61] sts.

Next row – Cast on 44 [48, 50, 54] sts, rib to end. 93 [103, 105, 115] sts.
Work 3 rows straight, ending with WS facing for next row.

Shape shoulder
Next row – Cast on 2 sts, rib to end. 95 [105, 107, 117] sts.
Work 5 rows straight.
Next row – Cast on 2 sts, rib to end. 97 [107, 109, 119] sts.
Work 5 rows straight, ending with WS facing for next row.

Shape neck
Next row – (WS) Cast off 10 [14, 16, 20] sts, rib to end.

87 [93, 93, 99] sts.
Next row – Rib to end.
Work 20 rows casting off 4 sts at beg of next and 9 foll alt rows.
47 [53, 53, 59] sts.
Work 7 rows casting off 3 sts at beg of next and 3 foll alt rows.
35 [41, 41, 47] sts.

Next row – (RS) (K1, K2tog, P1, P2tog) 4 times, K3, (P3, K3) 1 [2, 2, 3] times, P2. 27 [33, 33, 39] sts.

Next row – K2, P3, (K3, P3) 1 [2, 2, 3] times, (K2tog, P2tog) 4 times.
19 [25, 25, 31] sts.

Next row – Cast off 8 [14, 14, 20] sts, K to last 8 sts, P3, K3, P2.
Cast off rem 11 sts.

SLEEVES (Both alike)
Using 4mm needles cast on 79 [85, 91, 97]sts.

Row 1 – (RS) P2, ★ K3, P3, rep from ★ to last 5 sts, K3, P2.
Row 2 – K2, ★ P3, K3, rep from ★ to last 5 sts, P3, K2.
These 2 rows set rib.
Cont in rib shaping sides by inc 1 st at each end of 35th and foll 10th row then every foll 12th row to 97 [103, 109, 115] sts, working inc sts in rib.
Cont straight until sleeve meas 49 [50, 51, 51]cm, ending with RS facing for next row.

Shape top
Cast off 7 sts at beg of next 2 rows.
83 [89, 95, 101] sts.
Work 2 rows dec 1 st at each end of every row.
79 [85, 91, 97] sts.
Work 28 rows dec 1 st at each end of next and every foll alt row.
51 [57, 63, 69] sts.
Work 14 rows dec 1 st at each end of every row.
23 [29, 35, 41] sts.
Cast off 7 [9, 11, 13] sts at beg of next 2 rows.
Cast off rem 9 [11, 13, 15] sts.

FESCUE

MAKING UP
Press following instructions on ball band.
Join shoulder and side seams.
(Back is 1.5cm longer than fronts to allow for front edgings)

Left side edging
With RS facing using 4mm circular needle, beg at centre back neck,
pick up and knit 32 [32, 33, 33] sts from left side of back neck, 67 [67,
69, 69] sts down left side of neck, 19 [25, 25, 31] sts from cast off edge of
front and 64 [64, 70, 70] sts from bottom edge of left front.
182 [188, 197, 203] sts.
Next row – (WS) (P3, K3) 11 [11, 12, 12] times, P to end.
Next row – P to last 66 [66, 72, 72] sts, (P3, K3) 11 [11, 12, 12] times.
★ These 2 rows form rib and stocking stitch edging.
Work 2 rows more.
Cast off in rib for rib sts, and purlways for stocking stitch edging.

Right side edging
With RS facing using 4mm circular needle, beg at right side, pick up
and knit 64 [64, 70, 70] sts from bottom edge of right front,
19 [25, 25, 31] sts from cast off edge of front, 67 [67, 69, 69] sts up
right side of neck and 32 [32, 33, 33] sts from right side of back of neck
ending at centre of back neck. 182 [188, 197, 203] sts.
Next row – (WS) P to last 66 [66, 72, 72] sts, (K3, P3) 11 [11, 12, 12] times.
Next row – (K3, P3) 11 [11, 12, 12] times, K to end.
Work as given for left front edging from ★.
Join edgings to back at bottom of side seams.
Join sleeve seams reversing stitching on first 6cm for turn back cuff.
Insert sleeves.
Using photograph as a guide, sew 1 button to each front.
Tie
Using 4.00mm crochet hook make a chain 30cm long. Twist around
buttons to fasten.

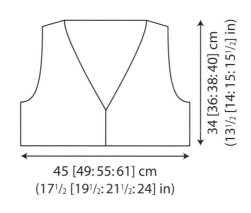

45 [49: 55: 61] cm
(17½ [19½: 21½: 24] in)

34 [36: 38: 40] cm
(13½ [14: 15: 15½] in)

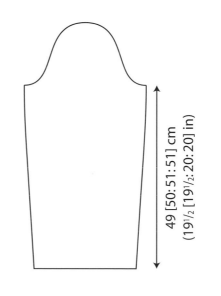

49 [50: 51: 51] cm
(19½ [19½: 20: 20] in)

HEATH
by Sarah Hatton
main image page 8

SIZE

	S	M	L	XL	
	8/10	12/14	16/18	20/22	
To fit bust					
	82-87	92-97	102-107	112-117	cm
	32-34	36-38	40-42	44-46	in

YARN

Rowan Tapestry

	10	10	11	12	x 50gm

NEEDLES

1 pair 4mm (no 8) (US 6) needles
Stitch holders

TENSION

22 sts and 32 rows to 10cm on 4mm (US 6) needles over pattern.

BACK
Using 4mm needles cast on 110 [120, 134, 148] sts.
Work 4 rows garter st.
Row 1 – (RS) Knit.
Row 2 – Purl.
Row 3 – Knit.
Row 4 – Purl.
Row 5 – Purl.
Row 6 – Purl.
Rows 7 to 12 – As rows 1 - 6.
Row 13 – Purl.
Row 14 – Purl.
These 14 rows form patt.
Cont in patt shaping sides by dec 1 st at each end of 5th [9th, 11th, 15th]
and 6 foll 8th rows. 96 [106, 120, 134] sts.
Work 15 rows straight.

Inc 1 st at each end of next and 4 foll 8th rows.
106 [116, 130, 144] sts.
Work 11 rows more, ending with RS facing for next row.
(Back should meas 41[42, 43, 44]cm)
Shape armholes
Cast off 6 [7, 8, 9] sts at beg of next 2 rows. 94 [102, 114, 126] sts.
Work 2 [4, 4, 4] rows dec 1 st at each end of every row.
90 [94, 106, 118] sts.
Work 4 [4, 8, 12] rows dec 1 st at each end of next and every foll alt
row. 86 [90, 98, 106] sts.
Work 5 [9, 9, 9] rows dec 1 st at each end of next and every foll 4th
row. 82 [84, 92, 100] sts.
Cont straight until armhole meas 21 [22, 23, 24]cm, ending with RS
facing for next row.

Shape shoulders
Cast off 6 [7, 7, 9] sts at beg of next 2 rows. 70 [72, 78, 82] sts.
Next row – Cast off 6 [6, 7, 9]sts, patt until there are
11 [11, 12, 13] sts on right hand needle, turn and work this side first.
Next row – Cast off 4 sts, patt to end.
Cast off rem 7 [7, 8, 9] sts.
With RS facing, rejoin yarn to rem sts, cast off centre
36 [36, 38, 38] sts, patt to end.
Complete to match first side reversing shapings.

LEFT FRONT
Using 4mm needles cast on 77 [82, 89, 96] sts.
Row 1 – (RS) K to last 16 sts, (P2, K3) 3 times, K1.
Row 2 – K1, (P3, K2) 3 times, K to end.
Row 3 – As Row 1.
Row 4 – As Row 2.
Rows 1 and 2 set rib patt for Front edging on the 16 sts.
Beg with Row 1 of patt as given for Back:-

HEATH

Next row – Patt to last 16 sts, slip 16 sts onto a stitch holder.
61 [66, 73, 80] sts.
Working on these 61 [66, 73, 80] sts only, cont in patt as given for back shaping side by dec 1 st at side edge (beg) in 18th [22nd, 24th, 28th] and 6 foll 8th rows. 54 [59, 66, 73] sts.
Work 11 [13, 13, 13] rows straight.
Shape neck
Work 48 [46, 46, 46] rows inc 1 st at side edge in 5th [3rd, 3rd, 3rd] and 4 foll 8th rows **at same time** dec 1 st at neck edge in next and every foll 4th row, ending with RS facing for next row.
47 [52, 59, 66] sts.
Shape armhole
Next row – Cast off 6 [7, 8, 9] sts, patt to last 2 [0, 0, 0] sts, patt2tog 1 [0, 0, 0] times. 40 [45, 51, 57] sts.
Work 1 row more.
Work 2 [4, 4, 4] rows dec 1 st at armhole edge in every row **at same time** dec 0 [1, 1, 1] st at neck edge in 0 [1st, 1st, 1st] of these rows.
38 [40, 46, 52] sts.
Work 4 [4, 8, 12] rows dec 1 st at armhole edge in next and every foll alt row **at same time** dec 1 st at neck edge in 1st and every foll 4th row. 35 [37, 40, 43] sts.
Work 5 [5, 9, 9] rows dec 1 st at armhole edge in next and every foll 4th row **at same time** dec 1 st at neck edge in next and every foll 4th row. 31 [33, 34, 36] sts.
Dec 1 st at neck edge only in every foll 4th row to 19 [21, 23, 27] sts.
Cont straight until front matches Back to shoulder ending with RS facing for next row.
Shape shoulder
Cast off 6 [6, 7, 9] sts at beg of next and foll alt row.
Work 1 row more.
Cast off rem 7 [7, 8, 9] sts.

RIGHT FRONT
Using 4mm needles cast on 77 [82, 89, 96] sts.
Row 1 – (RS) K1, (K3, P2) 3 times, K to end.
Row 2 – K to last 16 sts, (K2, P3) 3 times, K1.
Row 3 – As row 1.
Row 4 – As row 2.
Rows 1 and 2 set rib pattern for Front Edging on first 16 sts.
Next row – Patt and slip first 16 sts onto a stitch holder, beg with Row 1 of patt as set for Back, patt to end. 61 [66, 73, 80] sts.
Working on these 61 [66, 73, 80] sts only, complete as given for Left Front reversing shapings and working 1 row more before armhole and shoulder shaping.

SLEEVES (Both alike)
Using 4mm needles cast on 53 [58, 58, 63] sts.
Row 1 – (RS) ★ K3, P2, rep from ★ to last 3 sts. K3.
Row 2 – ★ P3, K2, rep from ★ to last 3 sts, P3.
These 2 rows form 3x2 rib.
Cont in rib until sleeve meas 8cm, dec 1 [4, 0, 3] sts evenly across last row and ending with RS facing for next row. 52 [54, 58, 60] sts.
Cont in patt as set for Back shaping sides by inc 1 st at each end of next and every foll 8th row to 80 [82, 86, 88] sts.
Cont straight until sleeve meas 46 [47, 48, 48]cm, ending with RS facing for next row.
Shape top
Cast off 6 [7, 8, 9] sts at beg of next 2 rows. 68 [68, 70, 70] sts.
Work 2 rows dec 1 st at each end of every row. 64 [64, 66, 66] sts.
Work 28 [28, 28, 32] rows dec 1 st at each end of next and every foll alt row.
36 [36, 38, 34] sts.
Work 4 [4, 8, 6] rows dec 1 st at each end of every row.

28 [28, 22, 22] sts.
Cast off 9 [9, 7, 7] sts at beg of next 2 rows.
Cast off rem 10 [10, 8, 8] sts.

MAKING UP
Join shoulder seams.
Left front edging
With RS facing rejoin yarn to 16 sts left on a stitch holder.
Row 1 – (RS) (P2, K3) 3 times, K1.
Row 2 – K1, (P3, K2) 3 times.
These 2 rows set 3x2 rib.
Cont in rib as set until edging is long enough when slightly stretched to fit up left front edge to centre back neck, ending with RS facing for next row. Cast off.
Slip stitch in place.
Right front edging
With WS facing rejoin yarn to 16 sts left on a stitch holder.

Row 1 – (WS) (K2, P3) 3 times, K1.
Row 2 – K1, (K3, P2) 3 times.
These 2 rows set 3x2 rib.
Complete as given for Left front edging, fitting up right front edge.
Join cast off edges of left and right front edging at centre back neck.
Pocket
Using 4mm needles cast on 22 sts.
Work 32 rows in patt as given for Back, ending with RS facing for next row.
Knit 1 row. Cast off.
Sew pocket on Right Front approx 6cm from side seam and 3cm from bottom edge.
Ties (Make 2)
Using 4mm needles cast on 44 sts. Cast off.
Sew 1 to right front edge at start of neck shaping and 1 to left side seam to correspond.

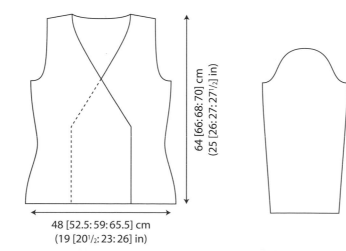

64 [66:68:70] cm
(25 [26:26:27:27½] in)

48 [52.5:59:65.5] cm
(19 [20½:23:26] in)

46 [47:48:48] cm
(18 [18½:19:19] in)

MARSH
by Marie Wallin

main image page 13

26

SIZE

	S	M	L	XL	
	8/10	12/14	16/18	20/22	
To fit bust					
	82-87	92-97	102-107	112-117	cm
	32-34	36-38	40-42	44-46	in

YARN

Rowan Tapestry

	9	10	11	12	x 50 gm

NEEDLES

1 pair 4mm (no 8) (US 6) needles

TENSION

22 sts and 30 rows to 10cm over stocking stitch on 4mm (US 6) needles

BACK AND FRONT (Both alike)

Using 4mm needles cast on 114 [124, 138, 150] sts.
Beg with a K row, work 8 rows in stocking stitch, ending with RS facing for next row.
Next row – Purl. ★
Beg with a P row cont in stocking stitch shaping sides by dec 1 st at each end of 22nd and every foll 16th row to 102 [112, 126, 138] sts.
Cont straight until work meas 39 [42, 43, 44]cm from P row, ending with RS facing for next row.

Shape armholes

Cast off 4 [5, 6, 7] sts at beg of next 2 rows. 94 [102, 114, 124] sts.
Work 2 [2, 4, 6] rows dec 1 st at each end of every row. 90 [98, 106, 112] sts.
Work 6 [8, 10, 10] rows dec 1 st at each end of next and every foll alt row. 84 [90, 96, 102] sts.
Work 9 rows dec 1 st at each end of next and 2 foll 4th rows. 78 [84, 90, 96] sts.
Cont straight until armholes meas 21 [22, 23, 24] cm, ending with RS facing for next row.

Shape shoulders

Cast off 5 [6, 6, 7] sts at beg of next 2 rows. 68 [72, 78, 82] sts.
Cast off 5 [6, 7, 8] sts at beg of next 2 rows. 58 [60, 64, 66] sts.
Cast off 3 [4, 5, 6] sts at beg of next 2 rows. 52 [52, 54, 54] sts.

Shape neck

Work 3 rows dec 1 st at each end of next and foll alt row. 48 [48, 50, 50] sts.
Work 21 rows straight, ending with RS facing for next row. Cast off.

SLEEVES (Both alike)

Using 4mm needles cast on 62 [64, 66, 68] sts.
Work as given for Back and Front to ★.
Beg with a P row cont in stocking stitch shaping sides by dec 1 st at each end of 8th and 2 foll 6th rows. 56 [58, 60, 62] sts.
Inc 1 st at each end of 10th and every foll 6th row to 74 [76, 78, 80] sts then every foll 8th row to 84 [86, 88, 90] sts.
Cont straight until sleeve meas 45[46, 47, 47]cm from P row, ending with RS facing for next row.

Shape top

Cast off 4 [5, 6, 7] sts at beg of next 2 rows. 76 sts.
Work 4 [2, 2, 2] rows dec 1 st at each end of every row. 68 [72, 72, 72] sts.

Size XL only

Work 16 rows dec 1 st at each end of next and every foll 4th row. 64 sts.

All sizes

Work 26 [34, 38, 24] rows dec 1 st at each end of next and every foll alt row. 42 [38, 34, 40] sts.
Work 8 [6, 4, 6] rows dec 1 st at each end of every row. 26 [26, 26, 28] sts.
Cast off 8 [8, 8, 9] sts at beg of next 2 rows.
Cast off rem 10 sts.

MAKING UP

Press following instructions given on ball band. Join shoulder and neck seams. Join side and sleeve seams. Insert sleeves.

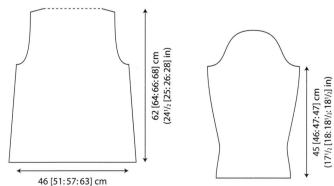

46 [51:57:63] cm
(18 [20: 22½: 25] in)

62 [64:66:68] cm
(24½ [25: 26:28] in)

45 [46:47:47] cm
(17½ [18: 18½: 18½] in)

MEADOW

by Sarah Hatton

main image page 9

28

SIZE

	8	10	12	14	16	18	
To fit bust							
	82	87	92	97	102	107	cm
	32	34	36	38	40	42	in

YARN

Rowan Tapestry

5	5	5	6	6	6 x 50gm

NEEDLES

1 pair each 4mm (no 8) (US 6) and 3¼ mm (no 10) (US 3) needles
Stitch holders

TENSION

22 sts and 30 rows to 10cm on 4mm (US 6) needles over stocking stitch

BACK

Using 3¼ mm needles cast on 98 [106, 110, 114, 122, 130] sts.
Row 1 – (RS) ★ K2, P2, rep from ★ to last 2 sts, K2.
Row 2 – P2, ★ K2, P2, rep from ★ to end.
These 2 rows form 2x2 rib.
Work 20 rows more in rib, dec 2 [4, 4, 2, 4, 4] sts evenly across last row.
96 [102, 106, 112, 118, 126] sts.
Change to 4mm needles.
Cont in st-st shaping sides by dec 1 st at each end of next and 4 foll 4th rows. 86 [92, 96, 102, 108, 116] sts.
Work 9 rows straight.
Inc 1 st at each end of next and 4 foll 8th rows.
96 [102, 106, 112, 118, 126] sts.
Cont straight until back meas 30.5 [30, 29.5, 32, 31.5, 33]cm, ending with RS facing for next row.
Shape armholes
Cast off 5 [6, 6, 7, 8, 9] sts at beg of next 2 rows.

86 [90, 94, 98, 102, 108] sts.
Work 2 [2, 2, 2, 2, 4] rows dec 1 st at each end of every row.
82 [86, 90, 94, 98, 100] sts.
Work 4 [6, 6, 8, 8, 8] rows dec 1 st at each end of next and every foll alt row. 78 [80, 84, 86, 90, 92] sts. ★★
Work 9 rows dec 1 st at each end of next and 2 foll 4th rows.
72 [74, 78, 80, 84, 86] sts.
Cont straight until armhole meas 19.5 [20, 20.5, 21, 21.5, 22]cm, ending with RS facing for next row.
Shape shoulders
Cast off 4 [5, 5, 6, 6, 6] sts at beg of next 2 rows.
64 [64, 68, 68, 72, 74] sts.
Next row – Cast off 5 [5, 6, 6, 6, 7] sts, K until there are
9 [9, 10, 10, 11, 11] sts on right hand needle, turn and work this side first.
Next row – Cast off 4 sts, P to end.
Cast off rem 5 [5, 6, 6, 7, 7] sts.
Slip centre 36 [36, 36, 36, 38, 38] sts onto a holder, rejoin yarn to rem sts, K to end.
Complete to match first side reversing shapings.

FRONT

Work as given for Back to ★★.
Divide for neck
Next row – K2tog, K30 [31, 33, 33, 35, 36], turn and work this side first.
Next row – P to end. 31 [32, 34, 34, 36, 37] sts.
Work 2 [2, 2, 0, 0, 0] rows dec 1 st at neck edge in every row.
29 [30, 32, 34, 36, 37] sts.
Work 8 [8, 6, 12, 12, 14] rows dec 1 st at armhole edge in next and foll 4th row **at same time** dec 1 st at neck edge in next and every foll alt row. 23 [24, 27, 26, 28, 28] sts.
Dec 1 st at neck edge only in next and every foll 4th row to

14 [15, 17, 18, 19, 20] sts.
Cont straight until armhole meas 19.5 [20, 20.5, 21, 21.5, 22]cm, ending with RS facing for next row.

Shape shoulder
Cast off 4 [5, 5, 6, 6, 6] sts at beg of next row and 5 [5, 5, 6, 6, 6, 7] sts at beg of foll alt row.
Work 1 row more.
Cast off rem 5 [5, 6, 6, 7, 7] sts.
Slip centre 14 [14, 14, 16, 16, 16] sts onto a holder.
With RS facing, rejoin yarn to rem sts and K to last 2 sts, K2tog.
31 [32, 34, 34, 36, 37] sts.
Complete to match first side reversing shapings, and working 1 row more before shoulder shaping.

MAKING UP
Join right shoulder seam.

Neck edging
With RS facing, using 3¼mm needles pick up and knit
34 [34, 34, 35, 36, 36] sts down left side of neck, knit across 14 [14, 14, 16, 16, 16] sts left on a stitch holder at front of neck, pick up and knit 34 [34, 34, 35, 36, 36] sts up right side of neck, 2 sts from right side of back neck, knit across 36 [36, 36, 36, 38, 38] sts left on a stitch holder at back of neck and pick up and knit 2 sts from left side of back neck.
122 [122, 122, 126, 130, 130] sts.
Beg with 2nd row of 2x2 rib, work 6 rows in rib.
Cast off in rib.
Join left shoulder and neck band seam.

Armhole edgings (Both alike)
With RS facing, using 3¼mm needles pick up and knit
90 [94, 98, 102, 102, 106] sts evenly around armhole edge.
Beg with 2nd row of 2x2 rib, work 6 rows in rib.
Cast off in rib.

Join side and armhole edging seams.

Belt tabs (Make 2)
Using 3¼ mm needles cast on 5 sts.
Work in garter st until tab meas 3 cm, ending with RS facing for next row.
Cast off.
Sew onto front of garment at waistline approx 5 cm from side seams.

Belt
Using 3¼mm needles cast on 7 sts.
Work in garter st until belt meas 125 [125, 125, 135, 135, 135]cm, ending with RS facing for next row.
Cast off.

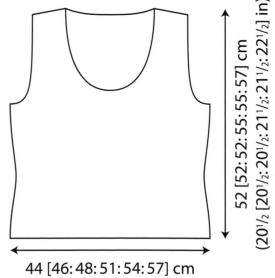

52 [52: 52: 55: 55: 57] cm
(20½ [20½: 20½: 21½: 21½: 22½] in)

44 [46: 48: 51: 54: 57] cm
(17½ [18: 19: 20: 21½: 22½] in)

MILLET
by Marie Wallin

main image page 12

MILLET

SIZE

	S	M	L	XL	
	8/10	12/14	16/18	20/22	

To fit bust

	82-87	92-97	102-107	112-117	cm
	32-34	36-38	40-42	44-46	in

YARN

Rowan Tapestry

	8	9	10	11	x 50gm

NEEDLES

1 Pair each 4mm (no 8) (US 6) and 3¼ mm (no 10) (US 3) needles
Stitch holders

TENSION

22 sts and 30 rows to 10cm on 4mm (UK8/USA6) needles over stocking stitch.

BACK

Using 3¼mm needles cast on 106 [118, 130, 146] sts.
Row 1 – (RS) ★ K2, P2, rep from ★ to last 2 sts, K2.
Row 2 – P2, ★ K2, P2, rep from ★ to end.
These 2 rows form 2x2 rib.
Work 52 rows more in rib, dec 3 [3, 3, 5] sts evenly across last row.
103 [115, 127, 141] sts.
Change to 4mm needles. ★★
Beg with a K row, cont in stocking stitch until back meas
47 [49, 51, 53]cm, ending with RS facing for next row.
Shape shoulders and back neck
Next row – Cast off 8 [9, 10, 10] sts, K until there are
20 [25, 29, 36] sts on right hand needle, turn and work this side first.

Next row – P2tog, P to end. 19 [24, 28, 35] sts.
Next row – Cast off 8 [9, 10, 11] sts, K to last 2 sts, K2tog.
10 [14, 17, 23] sts.
Next row – P2tog, P to end.
Cast off rem 9 [13, 16, 22] sts.
Slip centre 47 [47, 49, 49] sts onto a stitch holder
With RS facing rejoin yarn to rem sts, K to end.
Complete to match first side reversing shapings.

FRONT

Work as given for back to ★★.
Beg with a K row, cont in stocking stitch until front meas
37 [39, 40, 42]cm, ending with RS facing for next row.
Shape neck
Next row – K38 [44, 48, 55], turn and work this side first.
Next row – Purl.
Work 4 rows dec 1 st at neck edge in every row. 34 [40, 44, 51] sts.
Work 12 rows dec 1 st at neck edge in next and every foll alt row.
28 [34, 38, 45] sts.
Work 9 [9, 5, 5] rows dec 1 st at neck edge in next and 2 [2, 1, 1] foll 4th rows.
25 [31, 36, 43] sts.
Cont straight until front matches back to shoulder shaping, ending with RS facing for next row.
Shape shoulder
Cast off 8 [9, 10, 10] sts at beg of next and 8 [9, 10, 11] sts at beg of foll alt row.
Work 1 row more.
Cast off rem 9 [13, 16, 22] sts.
Slip centre 27 [27, 31, 31] sts onto a stitch holder, with RS facing, rejoin yarn to rem sts, K to end.

Complete to match first side reversing shapings and working 1 row more before shoulder shaping.

SLEEVES (Both alike)
Using 3¼mm needles cast on 58 [62, 62, 62] sts.
Work 41 rows in 2x2 rib as set for back, ending with WS facing for next row.
Next row – P1 [4, 3, 1] ★ inc in next st purlways, rep from ★ to last 1 [4, 3, 1] sts, P1 [4, 3, 1]. 114 [116, 118, 122]sts.
Change to 4mm needles.
Beg with a K row, cont in stocking stitch shaping sides by inc 1 st at each end of every foll 8th row to 132 [134, 136, 138] sts.
Cont straight until sleeve meas 46 [47, 48, 48]cm, ending with RS facing for next row.
Cast off.

MAKING UP
Join right shoulder seam.
Neckband
With RS facing using 3¼mm needles pick up and knit 23 [23, 24, 24] sts down left side of neck, knit across 27 [27, 31, 31] sts left on a stitch holder at front of neck, pick up and knit 23 [23, 24, 24] sts up right side of neck, 3 sts down right side of back neck, knit across 47 [47, 49, 49] sts left on a stitch holder at back of neck and pick up and knit 3 sts up left side of neck. 126 [126, 134, 134] sts.
Beg with row 2 of 2x2 rib, work 5 rows in rib. Cast off in rib.
Join left shoulder and neckband seam.
Join side and sleeve seams.
Insert sleeves.

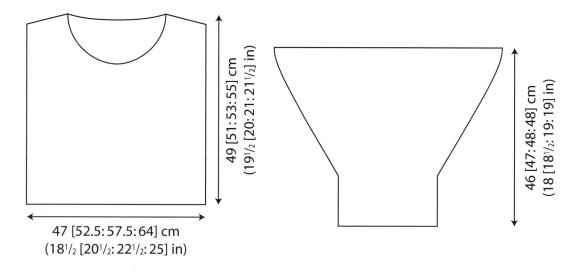

49 [51:53:55] cm
(19½ [20:21:21½] in)

47 [52.5:57.5:64] cm
(18½ [20½: 22½: 25] in)

46 [47:48:48] cm
(18 [18½: 19:19] in)

BERTIE GLOVES
by *Sarah Hatton*

main image page 15

YARN

Kid Classic

NEEDLES

1 pair 4½mm (no 7) (US 7) needles

TENSION

23 sts and 25 rows to 10cm over rib pattern on 4½mm (US 7) needles

FINGERLESS GLOVES
RIGHT GLOVE

Using 4½mm needles cast on 52 sts.

Row 1 – K1, ★ P2, K1, rep from ★ to end.
Row 2 – ★ P1, K2, rep from ★ to last st, P1.
These 2 rows rib cont in rib until work meas 25cm, ending with RS facing for next row. ★★
Shape thumb
Next row – Patt 26, inc in next st, K2, inc in next st, patt 22. 54 sts.
Work 3 rows.
Next row – Patt 26, inc in next st, K4, inc in next st, patt 22. 56 sts.
Work 3 rows.
Cont to increase in this way every 4th row to 60 sts.
Work 1 row.
Next row – Patt 38, turn, cast on 1 st.

Next row – Patt 13, cast on 1 st.
Work 6 rows on these 14 sts only.
Cast off.
Rejoin yarn to rem sts picking up 4 sts from base of thumb and patt to end.
Keeping patt as set, work 9 rows.
Cast off. Join side seam.

LEFT GLOVE
Work as given for Right glove to ★★
Shape thumb
Next row – Patt 22, inc in next st, K2, inc in next st, patt 26. 54 sts.
Work 3 rows.
Next row – Patt 22, inc in next st, K4, inc in next st, patt 26. 56 sts.
Work 3 rows.
Cont to increase in this way every 4th row to 60 sts.
Work 1 row.
Next row – Patt 34, turn, cast on 1 st.
Next row – Patt 13, cast on 1 st.
Work 6 rows on these 14 sts only.
Cast off.
Rejoin yarn to rem sts picking up 4 sts from base of thumb and patt to end.
Keeping patt as set, work 9 rows.
Cast off. Join side seam.

RYE

by Marie Wallin

main image page 6

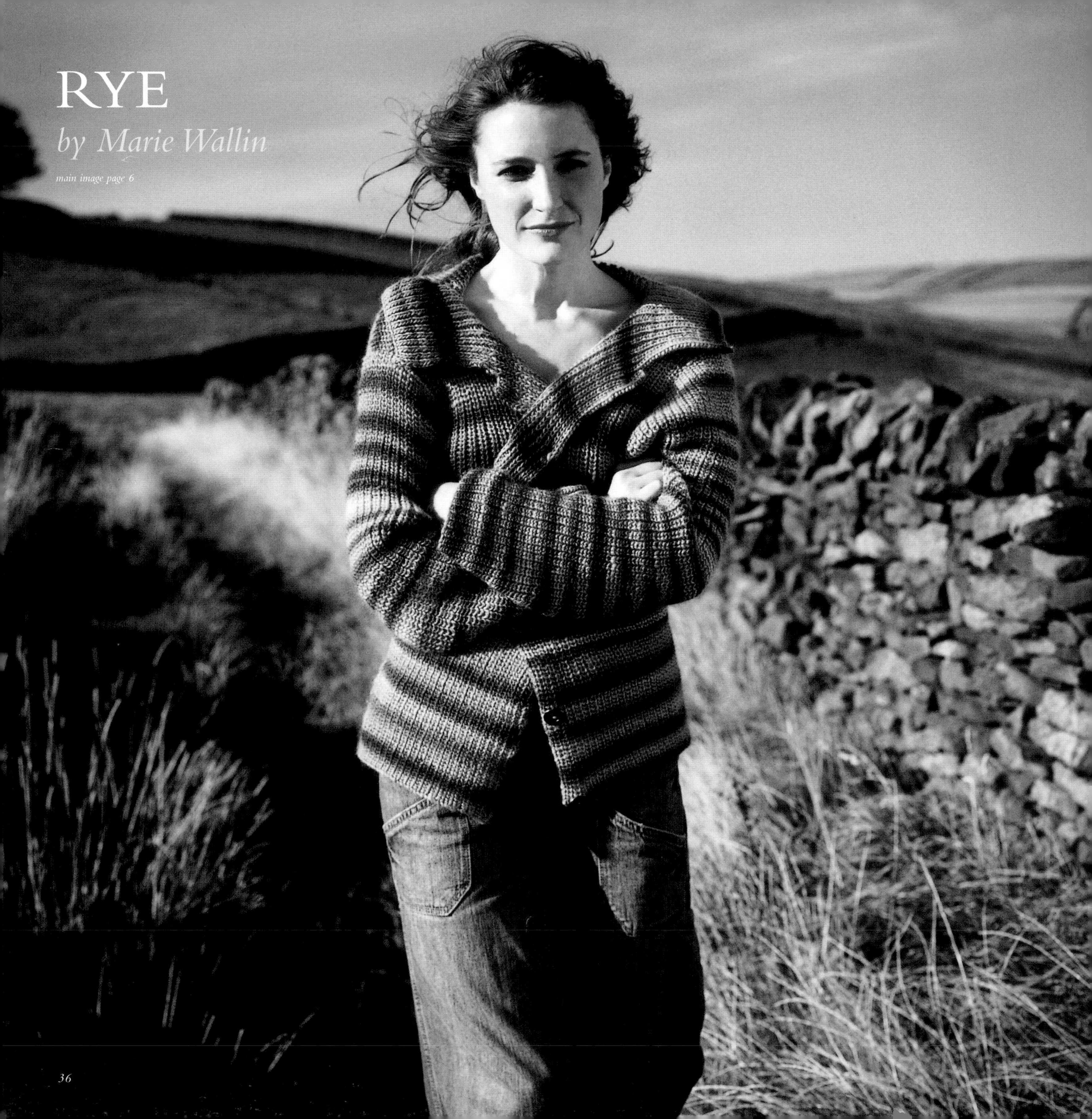

SIZE

	8	10	12	14	16	18	20	22	
To fit bust									
	82	87	92	97	102	107	112	117	cm
	32	34	36	38	40	42	44	46	in

YARN

Rowan Tapestry

	8	10	12	14	16	18	20	22	
	13	13	14	14	15	16	17	18	x 50gm

NEEDLES

1 pair 4mm (no 8) (US 6) needles

BUTTONS

6 x 00407

TENSION

23 sts and 43 rows to 10cm on 4mm (US 6) needles over pattern.

SPECIAL ABBREVIATION

K1B = Knit one st below – insert needle into st below next st on left hand needle and knit it in the usual way, slipping the st above off needle at same time.

BACK

Using 4mm needles cast on 101 [105, 111, 117, 125, 131, 139, 145] sts.
Row 1 – (RS) ★ K1, P1, rep from ★ to last st, K1.
Row 2 – P1, ★ K1B, P1, rep from ★ to end.
These 2 rows form patt.
Cont in patt shaping sides by dec 1 st at each end of 29th [29th, 29th, 35th, 35th, 37th, 37th, 37th] and 3 foll 10th rows.

93 [97, 103, 109, 117, 123, 131, 137] sts.
Work 19 rows straight.
Inc 1 st at each end of next and 3 foll 14th rows.
101 [105, 111, 117, 125, 131, 139, 145] sts.
Cont straight until back meas 33.5 [33, 32.5, 35, 34.5, 36, 35.5, 37]cm, ending with RS facing for next row.

Shape armholes

Cast off 4 [4, 5, 6, 7, 8, 9, 9] sts at beg of next 2 rows.
93 [97, 101, 105, 111, 115, 121, 127] sts.
Work 2 rows dec 1 st at each end of every row.
89 [93, 97, 101, 107, 111, 117, 123] sts.
Work 4 [6, 8, 8, 8, 8, 12, 10] rows dec 1 st at each end of next and every foll alt row.
85 [87, 89, 93, 99, 103, 105, 113] sts.
Work 5 [5, 5, 5, 9, 9, 9, 13] rows dec 1 st at each end of next and every foll 4th row.
81 [83, 85, 89, 93, 97, 99, 105] sts.
Cont straight until armhole meas 21.5 [22, 22.5, 23, 23.5, 24, 24.5, 25]cm, ending with RS facing for next row.

Shape shoulders

Cast off 6 [6, 7, 7, 8, 8, 9, 10] sts at beg of next 2 rows.
69 [71, 71, 75, 77, 81, 81, 85] sts.
Cast off 6 [7, 7, 8, 8, 9, 9, 10] sts at beg of next 2 rows.
57 [57, 57, 59, 61, 63, 63, 65] sts.
Cast off 7 [7, 7, 8, 8, 9, 9, 10] sts at beg of next 2 rows.
43 [43, 43, 43, 45, 45, 45, 45] sts.

Shape collar

Work 22 [22, 22, 22, 24, 24, 24, 24] rows inc 1 st at each end of 3rd and every foll alt row. 63 [63, 63, 63, 67, 67, 67, 67] sts.
Work 25 [25, 25, 25, 29, 29, 29, 29] rows inc 1 st at each end of next and every foll 4th row. 77 [77, 77, 77, 83, 83, 83, 83] sts.

RYE

Work 1 row more, ending with RS facing for next row.
Cast off.

LEFT FRONT
Using 4mm needles cast on 53 [55, 57, 61, 65, 69, 73, 75] sts.
Work in patt as set for back dec 1 st at side edge (beg) in
31st [31st, 31st, 37th, 37th, 39th, 39th, 39th] and 3 foll 10th rows.
49 [51, 53, 57, 61, 65, 69, 71] sts.
Work 19 rows straight.
Inc 1 st at side edge of next and 3 foll 14th rows.
53 [55, 57, 61, 65, 69, 73, 75] sts.
Cont straight until front matches back to armhole shaping, ending
with RS facing for next row.
Shape armhole
Next row – Cast off 4 [4, 5, 6, 7, 8, 9, 9] sts, patt to end.
49 [51, 52, 55, 58, 61, 64, 66] sts.
Work 2 rows dec 1 st at armhole edge in every row.
47 [49, 50, 53, 56, 59, 62, 64] sts.
Work 4 [6, 8, 8, 8, 8, 12, 10] rows dec 1 st at armhole edge in
next and every foll alt row. 45 [46, 46, 49, 52, 55, 56, 59] sts.
Work 5 [5, 5, 5, 9, 9, 9, 13] rows dec 1 st at armhole edge in next
and every foll 4th row. 43 [44, 44, 47, 49, 52, 53, 55] sts.
Cont straight until armhole matches back to shoulder shaping,
ending with RS facing for next row.
Shape shoulder
Next row – Cast off 6 [6, 7, 7, 8, 8, 9, 10] sts, patt to end.
37 [38, 37, 40, 41, 44, 44, 45] sts.
Next row – Patt to end.
Next row – Cast off 6 [7, 7, 8, 8, 9, 9, 10] sts, patt to end.
31 [31, 30, 32, 33, 35, 35, 35] sts.
Next row – (WS) Cast off 6 [6, 5, 6, 6, 7, 7, 6] sts, patt to end.

25 [25, 25, 26, 27, 28, 28, 29] sts.
Next row – Cast off 7 [7, 7, 8, 8, 9, 9, 10] sts, patt to end.
18 [18, 18, 18, 19, 19, 19, 19] sts.
Next row – Patt to end.
Shape collar
Work 22 [22, 22, 22, 24, 24, 24, 24] rows inc 1 st at side edge in
3rd and every foll alt row. 28 [28, 28, 28, 30, 30, 30, 30] sts.
Work 25 [25, 25, 25, 29, 29, 29, 29] rows inc 1 st at side edge in
next and every foll 4th row. 35 [35, 35, 35, 38, 38, 38, 38] sts.
Work 1 row more, ending with RS facing for next row.
Cast off.
Place markers for buttonholes 1 cm down from neck edge and
1 cm up from bottom edge and 4 more spaced evenly in between.

RIGHT FRONT
Using 4mm needles cast on 53 [55, 57, 61, 65, 69, 73, 75] sts.
Work as given for Left Front reversing all shapings and working
1 row more before shaping armhole and shoulders and 1 row less
before shaping collar and working buttonholes to correspond with
markers as follows:-
Buttonhole row – (RS) Patt2, yfwd, patt2tog, patt to end.

SLEEVES (Both alike)
Using 4mm needles cast on 51 [51, 53, 53, 55, 55, 57, 57] sts.
Cont in patt as set for back shaping side by inc 1 st at each end of
17th and every foll 28th row to 63 [63, 65, 65, 67, 67, 69, 69] sts.
Cont straight until sleeve meas 44 [44, 45, 45, 46, 46, 46, 45]cm,
ending with RS facing for next row.
Shape top
Cast off 4 [4, 5, 6, 7, 8, 9, 9] sts at beg of next 2 rows.
55 [55, 55, 53, 53, 51, 51, 51] sts.

38

Work 28 [28, 30, 30, 36, 36, 42, 42] rows dec 1 st at each end of next and every foll 4th [4th, 6th,6th,6th,6th,6th,6th] row.
41 [41, 45, 43, 41, 39, 37, 37] sts.
Work 12 [12, 10, 10, 18, 18, 16, 16] rows dec 1 st at each end of next and every foll alt row. 29 [29, 35, 33, 23, 21, 21, 21] sts.

For sizes 8 [10, 12, 14] only
Work 6 [6, 10, 10] rows dec 1 st at each end of every row.
17 [17, 15, 13] sts.

All sizes
Cast off 5 [5, 5, 4, 7, 7, 7, 7] sts at beg of next 2 rows.
Cast off rem 7 [7, 5, 5, 9, 7, 7, 7] sts.

MAKE UP
Join shoulder and collar seams.
Join side and sleeve seams.
Insert sleeves. Sew on buttons.

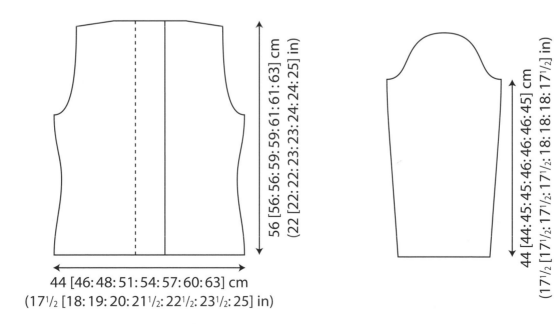

56 [56: 56: 59: 59: 61: 61: 63] cm
(22 [22: 22: 23: 23: 24: 24: 25] in)

44 [46: 48: 51: 54: 57: 60: 63] cm
(17^{1}/$_{2}$ [18: 19: 20: 21^{1}/$_{2}$: 22^{1}/$_{2}$: 23^{1}/$_{2}$: 25] in)

44 [44: 45: 45: 46: 46: 46: 45] cm
(17^{1}/$_{2}$ [17^{1}/$_{2}$: 17^{1}/$_{2}$: 17^{1}/$_{2}$: 18: 18: 18: 17^{1}/$_{2}$] in)

COUCH

by Sarah Hatton

main image page 7

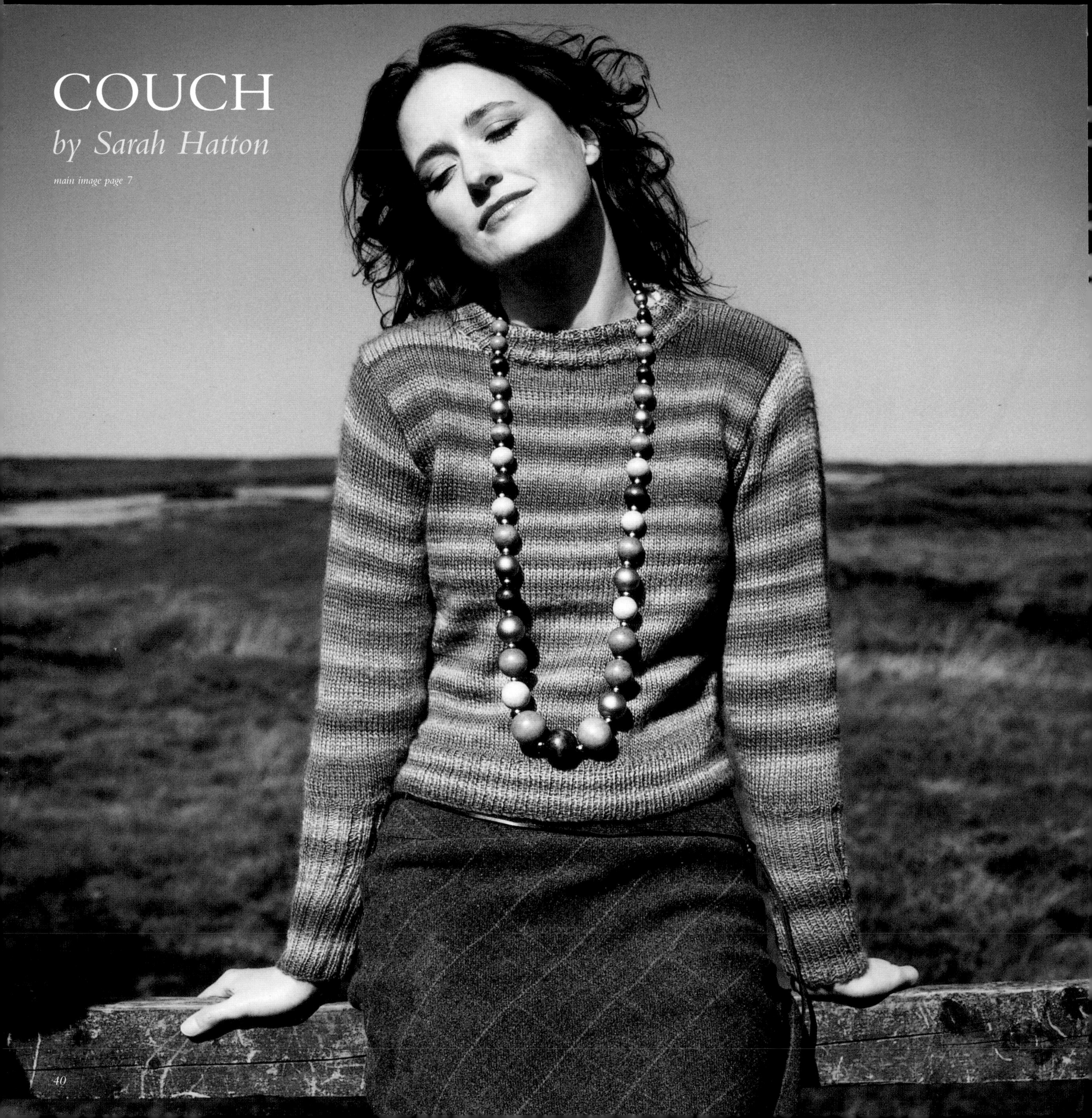

SIZE

	8	10	12	14	16	18	20	22	
To fit bust									
	82	87	92	97	102	107	112	117	cm
	32	34	36	38	40	42	44	46	in

YARN

Rowan Tapestry

	7	7	8	8	9	9	10	10	x 50gm

NEEDLES

1 pair 3¼ mm (no10) (US 3) needles
1 pair 4mm (no 8) (US 6) needles
Stitch holders

TENSION

22 sts and 30 rows to 10cm over stocking stitch on 4mm (US 6) needles.

BACK

Using 3¼mm needles cast on 99 [107, 111, 115, 123, 131, 135, 143] sts.
Row 1 – (RS) ★ K1, P1, rep from ★ to last st, K1.
Row 2 – P1, ★ K1, P1, rep from ★ to end.
These 2 rows form 1x1 rib.
Work 20 rows more in rib dec 3 [5, 5, 3, 5, 5, 3, 5] sts evenly across last of these rows.
96 [102, 106, 112, 118, 126, 132, 138] sts.
Change to 4mm needles.
Cont in st-st shaping sides by dec 1 st at each end of next and 4 foll 4th rows.
86 [92, 96, 102, 108, 116, 122, 128] sts.
Work 9 rows straight.
Inc 1 st at each end of next and 4 foll 8th rows.
96 [102, 106, 112, 118, 126, 132, 138] sts.
Cont straight until back meas 30.5 [30, 29.5, 32, 31.5, 33, 32.5, 34]cm, ending with RS facing for next row.
Shape armholes
Cast off 4 [4, 4, 5, 5, 6, 6, 7] sts at beg of next 2 rows.

88 [94, 98, 102, 108, 114, 120, 124] sts.
Work 2 [2, 2, 2, 4, 4, 4, 4] rows dec 1 st at each end of every row.
84 [90, 94, 98, 100, 106, 112, 116] sts.
Work 2 [4, 6, 8, 8, 8, 12, 12] rows dec 1 st at each end of next and every foll alt row.
82 [86, 88, 90, 92, 98, 100, 104] sts.
Work 5 [9, 9, 9, 5, 9, 9, 9] rows dec 1 st at each end of next and every foll 4th row.
78 [80, 82, 84, 88, 92, 94, 98] sts. ★★
Cont straight until armholes meas 19.5 [20, 20.5, 21, 21.5, 22, 22.5, 23]cm, ending with RS facing for next row.
Shape shoulders
Cast off 5 [6, 6, 6, 7, 7, 8, 8] sts at beg of next 2 rows.
68 [68, 70, 72, 74, 78, 78, 82] sts.
Next row – Cast off 6 [6, 6, 7, 7, 8, 8, 9] sts, K until there are 10 [10, 11, 11, 11, 12, 12, 13] sts on right hand needle, turn and work this side first.
Next row – Cast off 4 sts, P to end.
Cast off rem 6 [6, 7, 7, 7, 8, 8, 9] sts.
Leave centre 36 [36, 36, 36, 38, 38, 38, 38] sts on a stitch holder, with RS facing, rejoin yarn to rem sts and K to end.
Complete to match first side reversing shapings, working 1 row more before shoulder shaping.

FRONT

Work as given for Back to ★★.
Cont straight until armholes meas 14.5 [15, 15.5, 15, 15.5, 16, 15.5, 16]cm, ending with RS facing for next row.
Divide for neck
Next row – (RS) K25 [26, 27, 28, 29, 31, 32, 34], turn and work this side first.
Next row – Purl.
Work 2 rows dec 1 st at neck edge in every row.
23 [24, 25, 26, 27, 29, 30, 32] sts.
Work 11 rows dec 1 st at neck edge in next and every foll alt row.
17 [18, 19, 20, 21, 23, 24, 26] sts.
Cont straight until armhole meas 19.5 [20, 20.5, 21, 21.5, 22, 22.5, 23]cm,

ending with RS facing for next row.

Shape shoulder

Next row – Cast off 5 [6, 6, 6, 7, 7, 8, 8] sts, K to end.

12 [12, 13, 14, 14, 16, 16, 18] sts.

Next row – Purl.

Next row – Cast off 6 [6, 6, 7, 7, 8, 8, 9] sts, K to end.

Next row – Purl.

Cast off rem 6 [6, 7, 7, 7, 8, 8, 9] sts.

Leave centre 28 [28, 28, 28, 30, 30, 30, 30] sts on a stitch holder, with RS facing rejoin yarn to rem sts and K to end.

Complete to match first side reversing shapings, working 1 row more before shoulder shaping.

SLEEVES

Using 3¼ mm needles cast on 50 [50, 50, 50, 54, 54, 58, 58] sts.

Row 1 – (RS) ★ K2, P2, rep from ★ to last st, K2.

Row 2 – P2, ★ K2, P2, rep from ★ to end.

These 2 rows form 2x2 rib.

Work 64 rows more in 2x2 rib as given for Back dec 2 [2, 0, 0, 2, 2, 2, 2] sts evenly across last of these rows. 48 [48, 50, 50, 52, 52, 56, 56] sts.

Change to 4mm needles.

Cont in st-st shaping sides by inc 1 st at each end of next and every foll alt row to 62 [62, 64, 64, 66, 66, 70, 70] sts then on every foll 4th row to 84 [84, 86, 86, 88, 88, 92, 92] sts.

Cont straight until sleeve meas 45 [45, 46, 46, 47, 47, 46, 46]cm, ending with RS facing for next row.

Shape top

Cast off 4 [4, 4, 5, 5, 6, 6, 7] sts at beg of next 2 rows.

76 [76, 78, 76, 78, 76, 80, 78] sts.

Work 2 rows dec 1 st at each end of every row.

72 [72, 74, 72, 74, 72, 76, 74] sts.

Work 12 [12, 12, 12, 14, 14, 14, 14] rows dec 1 st at each end of next and every foll alt row. 60 [60, 62, 60, 60, 58, 62, 60] sts.

Work 12 rows dec 1 st at each end of every row.

36 [36, 38, 36, 36, 34, 38, 36] sts.

Cast off 12 [12, 13, 12, 12, 11, 13, 12] sts at beg of next 2 rows.

Cast off rem 12 sts.

MAKING UP

Join right shoulder seam.

Neckband

With RS facing, using 3¼ mm needles pick up and knit 15 [15, 15, 17, 17, 17, 19, 19] sts down left side of neck, knit across 28 [28, 28, 28, 30, 30, 30, 30] sts left on a stitch holder at front of neck, pick up and knit 15 [15, 15, 17, 17, 17, 19, 19] sts up right side of neck, 4 sts from right side of back neck, knit across 36 [36, 36, 36, 38, 38, 38, 38] sts left on a stitch holder at back of neck, pick up and knit 4 sts at left side of back neck. 102 [102, 102, 106, 110, 110, 114, 114] sts.

Beg with row 2 of 2x2 rib, work 11 rows in rib. Cast off in rib.

Join left shoulder and neckband seam.

Join side and sleeve seams.

Insert sleeves.

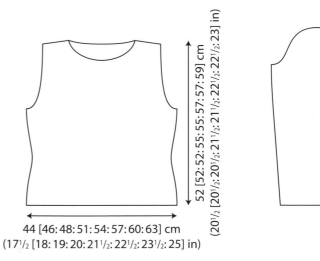

44 [46: 48: 51: 54: 57: 60: 63] cm
(17½ [18: 19: 20: 21½: 22½: 23½: 25] in)

52 [52: 52: 55: 55: 57: 57: 59] cm
(20½ [20½: 20½: 21½: 21½: 22½: 22½: 23] in)

45 [45: 46: 46: 47: 47: 46: 46] cm
(17½ [17½: 18: 18: 18½: 18½: 18: 18] in)

FOXTAIL

by Sarah Hatton

main image page 14

43

FOXTAIL

SIZE

	S	M	L	XL	
	8/10	12/14	16/18	20/22	
To fit bust					
	82–87	92–97	102–107	112–117	cm
	32–34	36–38	40–42	44–46	in

YARN

Rowan Tapestry

	6	7	8	9	x 50gm

NEEDLES

1 pair 4 mm (no 8) (US 6) needles
1 4mm (no 8) (US 6) circular needle

EXTRAS

1 x 00414 Kilt Pin

TENSION

22 sts and 30 rows to 10cm over stocking stitch on 4mm (US 6) needles

BACK AND FRONT YOKE (Knitted in 1 piece)
Using 4mm needles cast on 80 [82, 84, 84] sts.
Beg with a K row, cont in st-st shaping sides by inc 1 st at each end of 31st and foll 20th rows. 84 [86, 88, 88] sts.
Work 27 (29, 33, 33] rows straight, ending with RS facing for next row.
Place markers at each end of last row to denote top of right sleeve.
Work 42 [50, 58, 66] rows more, ending with RS facing for next row.
(Work should meas 40 [43, 47, 50]cm)
Divide for neck and right front
Next row – (RS) K40 [41, 42, 42], K2tog, turn and leave rem sts on a holder.
* **Next row –** (WS) Cast off 2 sts, P to end. 39 [40, 41, 41] sts.
Next row – Knit.
Rep from * twice. 35 [36, 37, 37] sts.
** **Next row –** Cast off 3 sts, P to end.
Next row – Knit. 32 [33, 34, 34] sts.

Rep from ** 9 times, 5 [6, 7, 7] sts.
Next row – P2tog, P3 [4, 5, 5].
Cast off rem 4 [5, 6, 6] sts.

Back
With RS facing, rejoin yarn to rem sts, K2tog, K to end.
41 [42, 43, 43] sts.
Next row – Purl.
Work 5 rows dec 1 st at back neck edge (beg) in next and every foll alt row. 38 [39, 40, 40] sts.
Work 43 [43, 47, 47] rows straight, ending with RS facing for next row.
Work 6 rows inc 1 st at back neck edge (beg) in next and every foll alt row. 41 [42, 43, 43] sts.
Leave these 41 [42, 43, 43] sts on a stitch holder.

Left front
Using 4 mm (US 6) needles cast on 4 [5, 6, 6] sts.
Next row – (RS) Knit.
Next row – Inc in first st, P 3 [4, 5, 5]. 5 [6, 7, 7] sts.
* **Next row –** K to end, cast on 3 sts.
Next row – Purl. 8 [9, 10, 10] sts.
Rep from * 9 times. 35 [36, 37, 37] sts.
** **Next row –** K to end, cast on 2 sts.
Next row – Purl. 37 [38, 39, 39] sts.
Rep from ** twice. 41 [42, 43, 43] sts.
Next row – K40 [41, 42, 42], inc in next st, then with RS facing, working on 41 [42, 43, 43] sts left on a stitch holder, inc in next st, K40 [41, 42, 42]. 84 [86, 88, 88] sts.
Beg with a P row, work 41 [49, 57, 65] rows more in st-st, ending with RS facing for next row. (Work should meas 73 [79, 87, 92]cm)
Place markers at each end of last row to denote top of left sleeve.
Cont shaping sides by dec 1 st at each end of 29th [31st, 35th, 35th] and foll 20th rows.
80 [82, 84, 84] sts.
Work 29 rows more, ending with RS facing for next row.
Cast off.

BOTTOM PANEL

Using 4 mm (US 6) circular needle cast on 224 [244, 272, 300] sts.
Beg with a K row and working in rows, work 20 rows st st, ending with RS facing for next row.

Next row – (RS) K54 [59, 66, 73], K2tog, Sl 1, K1, psso, K108 [118, 132, 146], K2tog, Sl 1, K1, psso, K54 [59, 66, 73]. 220 [240, 268, 296] sts.
Work 19 rows straight.

Next row – (RS) K53 [58, 65, 72], K2tog, Sl 1, K1, psso, K106 [116, 130, 144], K2tog, Sl 1, K1, psso, K 53 [58, 65, 72]. 216 [236, 264, 292] sts.
Work 19 rows straight.

Next row – (RS) K52 [57, 64, 71], K2tog, Sl 1, K1, psso, K104 [114, 128, 142], K2tog, Sl 1, K1, psso, K52 [57, 64, 71]. 212 [232, 260, 288] sts.
Work 19 rows straight.

Next row – (RS) K51 [56, 63, 70], K2tog, Sl 1, K1, psso, K102 [112, 126, 140], K2tog, Sl 1, K1, psso, K51 [56, 63, 70]. 208 [228, 256, 284] sts.
Cont straight until panel meas 32 [34, 36, 38]cm, ending with RS facing for next row. Cast off.

MAKING UP

Join sleeve seams from cast on edge to first set of markers and from cast off edge to second set of markers.
Join bottom panel to back and front yokes, matching front edges.

Front edging

With RS facing, using 4mm (US 6) circular needle, pick up and knit 70 [75, 79, 84] sts evenly along right front edge of bottom panel, 40 [40, 42, 42] sts up shaped edge, 30 [30, 34, 34] sts from back neck, 40 [40, 42, 42] sts down shaped edge and 70 [75, 79, 84] sts along left front edge of bottom panel.
250 [260, 276, 286] sts.
Beg with a P row, work 3 rows in st-st.

Next row – (Buttonhole row) K68 [73, 77, 82], cast off 2 sts (2 sts to be cast on over these 2 sts on next row), K to end.
Work 3 rows more.
Cast off. Sew on button.

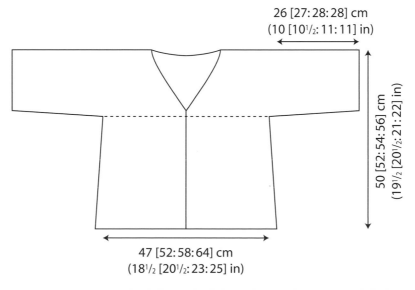

26 [27:28:28] cm
(10 [10½:11:11] in)

50 [52:54:56] cm
(19½ [20½:21:22] in)

47 [52:58:64] cm
(18½ [20½:23:25] in)

INFORMATION

TENSION

Obtaining the correct tension is perhaps the single factor which can make the difference between a successful garment and a disastrous one. It controls both the shape and size of an article, so any variation, however slight, can distort the finished garment.

Different designers feature in our books and it is **their** tension, given at the **start** of each pattern, which you must match. We recommend that you knit a square in pattern and/or stocking stitch (depending on the pattern instructions) of perhaps 5 - 10 more stitches and 5 - 10 more rows than those given in the tension note. Mark out the central 10cm square with pins. If you have too many stitches to 10cm try again using thicker needles, if you have too few stitches to 10cm try again using finer needles. Once you have achieved the correct tension your garment will be knitted to the measurements indicated in the size diagram shown at the end of the pattern.

SIZING & SIZE DIAGRAM NOTE

The instructions are given for the smallest size. Where they vary, work the figures in brackets for the larger sizes. **One set of figures refers to all sizes.** Included with most patterns in this brochure is a **'size diagram'**, or sketch of the finished garment and its dimensions. The size diagram shows the finished width of the garment at the under-arm point, and it is this measurement that the knitter should choose first; a useful tip is to measure one of your own garments which is a comfortable fit. Having chosen a size based on width, look at the corresponding length for that size; if you are not happy with the total length which we recommend, adjust your own garment before beginning your armhole shaping – any adjustment after this point will mean that your sleeve will not fit into your garment easily – don't forget to take your adjustment into account if there is any side seam shaping. Finally, look at the sleeve length; the size diagram shows the finished sleeve measurement, taking into account any top-arm insertion length. Measure your body between the centre of your neck and your wrist, this measurement should correspond to half the garment width plus the sleeve length. Again, your sleeve length may be adjusted, but remember to take into consideration your sleeve increases if you do adjust the length – you must increase more frequently than the pattern states to shorten your sleeve, less frequently to lengthen it.

FINISHING INSTRUCTIONS

After working for hours knitting a garment, it seems a great pity that many garments are spoiled because such little care is taken in the pressing and finishing process. Follow the following tips for a truly professional-looking garment.

PRESSING

Block out each piece of knitting and following the instructions on the ball band press the garment pieces, omitting the ribs. Tip: Take special care to press the edges, as this will make sewing up both easier and neater. If the ball band indicates that the fabric is not to be pressed, then covering the blocked out fabric with a damp white cotton cloth and leaving it to stand will have the desired effect. Darn in all ends neatly along the selvage edge or a colour join, as appropriate.

STITCHING

When stitching the pieces together, remember to match areas of colour and texture very carefully where they meet. Use a seam stitch such as back stitch or mattress stitch for all main knitting seams and join all ribs and neckband with mattress stitch, unless otherwise stated.

CONSTRUCTION

Having completed the pattern instructions, join left shoulder and neckband seams as detailed above. Sew the top of the sleeve to the body of the garment using the method detailed in the pattern, referring to the appropriate guide:

Shallow set-in sleeves: Match decreases at beg of armhole shaping to decreases at top of sleeve. Sew sleeve head into armhole, easing in shapings.

Set- in sleeves: Place centre of cast-off edge of sleeve to shoulder seam. Set in sleeve, easing sleeve head into armhole.

Join side and sleeve seams.

Slip stitch pocket edgings and linings into place.

Sew on buttons to correspond with buttonholes. Ribbed welts and neckbands and any areas of garter stitch should not be pressed.

EASY, STRAIGHT FORWARD KNITTING ☐

SUITABLE FOR THE AVERAGE KNITTER ☐ ☐

K – Knit	**foll** – following	**mm** – millimetres
P – Purl	**rem** – remain(ing)	**cm** – centimetres
st(s) – stitch(es)	**rev st-st** – reverse stocking stitch (1 row P, 1 row K)	**in(s)** – inch(es)
inc – increas(e)(ing)		**RS** – right side
dec – decreas(e)(ing)	**rep** – repeat	**WS** – wrong side
st-st – stocking Stitch (1 row K, 1 row P)	**alt** – alternate	**meas** – measures
	cont – continue	**yfwd** – yarn forward
g st – garter Stitch - (K every row)	**Sl 1** – slip one stitch	**yrn** – yarn round needle
	patt – pattern	
beg – begin(ning)	**tog** – together	

m1 – by picking up horizontal loop lying before next st and knitting in to back of it

tbl – through back of loop

m1P – by picking up horizontal loop lying before next st and purling info back of it

SIZING GUIDE

- Our sizing now conforms to standard clothing sizes. Therefore if you buy a standard size 12 in clothing, then our size 12 or Medium patterns will fit you perfectly.

- Dimensions in the charts below are body measurements, not garment dimensions, therefore please refer to the measuring guide to help you to determine which is the best size for you to knit.

MEASURING GUIDE

For maximum comfort and to ensure the correct fit when choosing a size to knit, please follow the tips below when checking your size.

Measure yourself close to your body, over your underwear and don't pull the tape measure too tight!

Bust/chest – measure around the fullest part of the bust/chest and across the shoulder blades.

Waist – measure around the natural waistline, just above the hip bone.

Hips – measure around the fullest part of the bottom.

If you don't wish to measure yourself, note the size of a favourite jumper that you like the fit of. Our sizes are now comparable to the clothing sizes from the major high street retailers, so if your favourite jumper is a size Medium or size 12, then our casual size Medium and standard size 12 should be approximately the same fit.

To be extra sure, measure your favourite jumper and then compare these measurements with the size diagram given at the end of the individual instructions.

Finally, once you have decided which size is best for you, please ensure that you achieve the tension required for the design you wish to knit. Remember if your tension is too loose, your garment will be bigger than the pattern size and you may use more yarn. If your tension is too tight, your garment could be smaller than the pattern size and you will have yarn left over. Furthermore if your tension is incorrect, the handle of your fabric will be too stiff or floppy and will not fit properly. It really does make sense to check your tension before starting every project.

STANDARD SIZING GUIDE FOR WOMEN

UK SIZE	8	10	12	14	16	18	20	22	
USA Size	6	8	10	12	14	16	18	20	
EUR Size	34	36	38	40	42	44	46	48	
To fit bust	32	34	36	38	40	42	44	46	inches
	82	87	92	97	102	107	112	117	cm
To fit waist	24	26	28	30	32	34	36	38	inches
	61	66	71	76	81	86	91	96	cm
To fit hips	34	6	38	40	42	44	46	48	inches
	87	92	97	102	107	112	117	122	cm

CASUAL SIZING GUIDE FOR WOMEN

As there are some designs that are intended to fit more generously, we have introduced our casual sizing guide. The designs that fall into this group can be recognised by the size range: Small, Medium, Large & Xlarge. Each of these sizes cover two sizes from the standard sizing guide, ie. Size S will fit sizes 8/10, size M will fit sizes 12/14 and so on. The sizing within this chart is also based on the larger size within the range, ie. M will be based on size 14.

	S	M	L	XL	
UK SIZE					
DUAL SIZE	8/10	12/14	16/18	20/22	
To fit bust	32 – 34	36 – 38	40 – 42	44 – 46	inches
	82 – 87	92 – 97	102 – 107	112 – 117	cm
To fit waist	24 – 26	28 – 30	32 – 34	36 – 38	inches
	61 – 66	71 – 76	81 – 86	91 – 96	cm
To fit hips	34 – 36	38 – 40	42 – 44	46 – 48	inches
	87 – 92	97 – 102	107 – 112	117 – 122	cm

BUST

WAIST

HIPS

AUSTRALIA: Australian Country Spinners, 314 Albert Street, Brunswick, Victoria 3056 *Tel:* (61) 3 9380 3888 *Fax:* (61) 3 9387 2674 *Email:* sales@auspinners.com.au

AUSTRIA: Coats Harlander GmbH, Autokaderstrasse 31, A -1210 Wien. *Tel:* (01) 27716 – 0 *Fax:* (01) 27716 - 228

BELGIUM: Pavan, Meerlaanstraat 73, B9860 Balegem (Oosterzele). *Tel:* (32) 9 221 8594 *Fax:* (32) 9 221 8594 *Email:* pavan@pandora.be

CANADA: Diamond Yarn, 9697 St Laurent, Montreal, Quebec, H3L 2N1. *Tel:* (514) 388 6188

Diamond Yarn (Toronto), 155 Martin Ross, Unit 3, Toronto, Ontario, M3J 2L9. *Tel:* (416) 736 6111 *Fax:* (416) 736 6112 *Email:* diamond@diamondyarn.com *Inernet:* www.diamondyarn.com

DENMARK: Coats Danmark A/S, Marienlunds Allé 4, 7430 Ikast. *Tel:* (45) 96 60 34 00 *Fax:* (45) 96 60 34 08 *Email:* coats@coats.dk

FINLAND: Coats Opti Oy, Ketjutie 3, 04220 Kerava *Tel:* (358) 9 274 871 *Fax:* (358) 9 2748 7330 *Email:* coatsopti.sales@coats.com

FRANCE: Coats France / Steiner Frères, 100, avenue du Général de Gaulle, 18 500 Mehun-Sur-Yèvre. *Tel:* (33) 02 48 23 12 30 *Fax:* (33) 02 48 23 12 40

GERMANY: Coats GMbH, Kaiserstrasse 1, D-79341 Kenzingen. *Tel:* (49) 7644 8020 *Fax:* (49) 7644 802399 Internet: www.coatsgmbh.de

HOLLAND: de Afstap, Oude Leliestraat 12, 1015 AW Amsterdam. *Tel:* (31) 20 6231445 *Fax:* (31) 20 427 8522

HONG KONG: East Unity Co Ltd, Unit B2, 7/F Block B, Kailey Industrial Centre, 12 Fung Yip Street, Chai Wan. *Tel:* (852) 2869 7110 *Fax:* (852) 2537 6952 *Email:* eastuni@netvigator.com

ICELAND: Storkurinn, Laugavegi 59, 101 Reykjavik. *Tel:* (354) 551 8258 *Email:* malin@mmedia.is

ITALY: D.L. srl, Via Piave, 24 – 26, 20016 Pero, Milan. *Tel:* (39) 02 339 10 180 *Fax:* (39) 02 33914661

JAPAN: Puppy-Jardin Co Ltd, 3-8-11 Kudanminami Chiyodaku, Hiei Kudan Bldg. 5F, Tokyo. *Tel:* (81) 3 3222-7076 *Fax:* (81) 3 3222- 7066 *Email:* info@rowan-jaeger.com

KOREA: Coats Korea Co Ltd, 5F Kuckdong B/D, 935-40 Bangbae- Dong, Seocho-Gu, Seoul. *Tel:* (82) 2 521 6262 *Fax:* (82) 2 521 5181

LEBANON: y.knot, Saifi Village, Mkhalissiya Street 162, Beirut. *Tel:* (961) 1 992211 *Fax:* (961) 1 315553 *Email:* y.knot@cyberia.net.lb

NEW ZEALAND: Please contact Rowan for details of stockists

NORWAY: Coats Knappehuset AS, Pb 100 Ulste, 5873 Bergen. *Tel:* (47) 55 53 93 00 *Fax:* (47) 55 53 93 93

SINGAPORE: Golden Dragon Store, 101 Upper Cross Street #02-51, People's Park Centre, Singapore 058357. *Tel:* (65) 6 5358454 *Fax:* (65) 6 2216278 *Email:* gdscraft@hotmail.com

SOUTH AFRICA: Arthur Bales PTY, PO Box 44644, Linden 2104. *Tel:* (27) 11 888 2401 *Fax:* (27) 11 782 6137

SPAIN: Oyambre, Pau Claris 145, 80009 Barcelona. *Tel:* (34) 670 011957 *Fax:* (34) 93 4872672 *Email:* oyambre@oyambreonline.com

SWEDEN: Coats Expotex AB, Division Craft, Box 297, 401 24 Goteborg. *Tel:* (46) 33 720 79 00 *Fax:* 46 31 47 16 50

SWITZERLAND: Coats Stroppel AG, CH -5300 Turgi (AG). *Tel:* (41) 562981220 *Fax:* (41) 56 298 12 50

TAIWAN: Laiter Wool Knitting Co Ltd, 10-1 313 Lane, Sec 3, Chung Ching North Road, Taipei. *Tel:* (886) 2 2596 0269 *Fax:* (886) 2 2598 0619

U.S.A.: Westminster Fibers Inc, 4 Townsend West, Suite 8, Nashua, New Hampshire 03063. *Tel:* (1 603) 886 5041 / 5043 *Fax:* (1 603) 886 1056 *Email:* rowan@westminsterfibers.com

U.K: Rowan, Green Lane Mill, Holmfirth, West Yorkshire, England HD9 2DX. *Tel:* +44 (0) 1484 681881 *Fax:* +44 (0) 1484 687920 *Email:* mail@knitrowan.com *Inernet:* www.knitrowan.com

For stockists in all other countries please contact Rowan for details.